Finger-Picking Styles for GUITAR

BY HAPPY TRAUM

Descriptive analysis and transcriptions of
traditional styles (in standard notation and
tablature) from the playing of
ETTA BAKER
ELIZABETH COTTEN
MISSISSIPPI JOHN HURT
BLIND LEMON JEFFERSON
SAM McGEE
PETE SEEGER
JOSEPH SPENCE
MERLE TRAVIS
DAVE VAN RONK
DOC WATSON

OAK PUBLICATIONS
LONDON/NEW YORK

MUSIC SALES LIMITED
78 NEWMAN STREET
LONDON WEST 1, ENGLAND

Music Transcribed by Happy Traum
Book Design by Jean Hammons and Ethel Raim

© 1966 Oak Publications

Music Sales Ltd.,
78 Newman Street, London W.1

Library of Congress Card Catalogue # 66-19052

ISBN 0-8256-0005-7

Printed in England by Compton Printing Limited
London and Aylesbury.

CONTENTS

Photo by Suzanne Szasz

Happy Traum

In 1953, when I was 15, a friend of mine played some records of Pete Seeger, Woody Guthrie, and Leadbelly. Someone else dragged me to a Peoples Artists Hootenanny, and before long I was blistering my fingers on a steel-stringed guitar with an action so high you could slip your hand between the strings and the fingerboard with room to spare. For three years I hardly missed a warm Sunday at Washington Square, and when the weather got cold we crowded into the Labor Temple on 14th Street and sang and picked til we were turned out, had supper (sometimes), and continued at someone's apartment on Spring Street til we were turned out. I made friends in those singing days that I still feel close to. Some never touch a guitar anymore, and a few are among the "big names" in the new folk - show business field.

When I first started playing the guitar, I studied with Walter Raim, who got me off to a good start. Later, when I became interested in blues, I studied with Brownie McGhee, which was a wonderful experience. We would just sit and pick, and I would stop him from time to time to find out how or why he did something or other. The runs, breaks, and songs I learned from him were not nearly as important as was the opportunity to play with someone who could give me a solid feeling for the blues.

Brownie was a tremendous influence on my music.

I recently spent a year studying classical guitar with Gustavo Lopez, the great Mexican guitarist, and I learned something about reading and writing music for the guitar, as well as the "correct" methods of playing.

With all of this, I still feel that Washington Square, and the people I met there, did more for my playing and love for folk music than any formal study could have done. I remember watching and playing with people like Tom Paley, Erik Darling, John Cohen, Ralph Rinzler, Eric Weissberg, Dick Weissman, Carl Granich, and many other young people who spurred the urban folksong movement. It was through these people, too, that I started listening to the people about whom I wrote this book.

My purpose in writing all this is two-fold: first, to let you know a little about myself, and second, to encourage you to play with, and listen to, as many people as possible. Be like a sponge, soaking up all you can learn from those around you, and yet give to those who want to learn from you. This kind of cooperation is one of the exciting things about the folk-learning process.

Introduction

Among students of folk guitar, the most popular and exciting style of playing is undoubtedly that style usually called "Travis picking", but also variously known as "two-finger picking", "three-finger picking", "Cotten picking", and just plain "picking". Whether swinging along with a bouncy ragtime tune or quietly rippling behind a pretty ballad, the sound is distinctive. It has a groove all its own, and once you've heard it you can't mistake the steady thump of the bass strings and the bright syncopation of the treble. It has become the goal towards which so many aspiring instrumentalists work, and once it is perfected there are endless possibilities for growth and exploration.

This particular style of playing seems to have started among Negro folk musicians just after the turn of the century, probably in imitation of the ragtime piano styles being played then, with its stride bass and free right hand syncopations. The fact that it was primarily a Negro style did not stop it from transcending racial barriers, and many of the white folk musicians who play this way learned directly from Negro guitarists. The interplay between white and Negro folk music was (and still is) a dominant force in creating the American folk styles as we know them, and the picking styles that concern us in this book are notable examples of that fact.

In order to help the student learn just what is happening in traditional picking styles, I have transcribed several outstanding examples from the recordings of some of the best and most influential exponents of this style. It is hoped that the student will learn these transcriptions not merely to imitate, but to be able to get inside the style and develop his own creative approach to picking. Among the numbers of fine folk guitarists, each one has a distinctive, unique way of playing.

It is not necessary to play every piece here note for note exactly as transcribed. It is much more important to get the feel of the style, and play the piece your own way. Try to get to concerts as much as possible to see and hear these artists in person. After all, this is a living and vital art form, and the printed page is a poor substitute for the real thing.

Listen to records! Everything transcribed in this book has been taken from a recording, noted with the comments about the piece. More important than listening to the particular tune at hand, though, is to listen to many other things by the same person, so that you can get a real feeling for his work; his singing and playing style, his "sound", his culture, and his personality. Folk music is an oral tradition still, even if you are learning only indirectly, through the person's recordings.

Use the transcriptions as a guide to enable you to figure out passages that you can't get by just listening. Always supplement the transcription by listening to the record, because there are things for which we have no printed language.

Note on reading the tablature:

The guitar tablature provided here is a substitute for (or a supplement to) the standard musical notation. The six lines represent the six strings of the guitar, with the bass E as the bottom line.

The number on the line is the fret at which the left hand finger stops the string. Thus, a C chord would be shown as

Two notes tied together with the letter H in between indicates a "hammer-on":

P is a "pull-off" (left hand pluck):

S is a slide from one fret to another, or to a fret from an optional point below it:

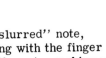

~ indicates a "choked" or "slurred" note, produced by stretching the string with the finger that is fretting it, thus raising the note, making a whining blue-note effect. A note can be raised a half tone or more this way.

Occasionally it is necessary to notate which right hand finger picks a string, and these are designated by the letters T (thumb), I (index), M (middle) and R (ring).

Starting To Pick

The basis of traditional finger picking styles is the "independent thumb", keeping a steady (usually 4/4) beat regardless of what the other fingers are doing. The first (or first and second) finger picks out the melody notes, sometimes playing them on the beat along with the bass, and sometimes off the beat, by putting the note between beats. The syncopated note can come either before or after the bass note. It is this syncopated melody against the steady bass that gives it such a distinctive (and swingy) sound.

Let's take a simple tune to illustrate this principle. We'll try Skip to My Lou for a start. Fretting a C chord, start your right thumb alternating between the 5th and the 4th strings in a steady rhythm, counting 1-2-3-4- 1-2-3-4 . Your first finger will be playing the melody while your thumb keeps up that steady bass. Of course, the bass notes will change with the change of chord. The melody notes are always found within or near the chord you're fretting. First, we'll play the melody on the beat throughout, without any syncopation:

Skip To My Lou

Now let's take some of the melody notes and put them **off** the beat:

Make sure that the change in the rhythm of the melody does not throw the steady bass off. As you can see, it is not hard to keep a steady bass going, and the melody is simple. It's putting the two different things together that will take practice.

Pattern Picking

Many guitar students start picking by learning a preset right hand pattern (I call this "pattern picking") that remains virtually unchanged throughout a song. Although none of the guitarists represented here use this type of playing, it has many advantages as well as disadvantages, and is used so widely (among city pickers) that it deserves some discussion.

The most well known pattern (usually misnamed "Travis picking") goes like this:

Finger a C chord. Now, your right hand thumb will alternate between the 5th string and the 3rd string, while your index and middle fingers alternate on the 2nd and 1st strings respectively. All together, the pattern is:

```
T  I T M T I T      T I T M T I T
M                   M
```

In standard tablature, it looks like this:

Notice where the accented beats are. This is what gives it that nice syncopated bounce. The thumb is playing a steady 4/4 beat, while the index and middle fingers are providing the on-beat, off-beat trebel. If you were playing a tune, the <u>middle finger</u> would carry most of the melody notes. This pattern has to be played over and over until it is fast, smooth, and automatic.

Although it looks complicated at first, this and other patterns can be learned with a few hours of practice, and the results can seem spectacular. It is pleasant to listen to, and it seems (to yourself and others) as if you are doing something that is very advanced. The trouble is, you can often get set in this pattern, and find yourself in a rut that's hard to break out of. It can be very useful, though, and certainly worth learning, if you remember that an unchanged pattern can get very boring after awhile, and that it is not the last word in picking!

Once you have mastered the above pattern, try using it as an accompaniment to some songs. <u>Pretty Peggy-o</u>, <u>Old Blue</u>, <u>Freight Train</u>, and <u>Don't Think Twice</u> come to my mind as possibilities, but you can use your own judgement as to where it fits best.

There are several minor variations of this pattern, such as:

```
T  I T M T I T   or T    T I T M T I or T T M T I T
                       M                    M
C
```

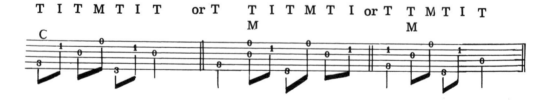

These changes may seem insignificant, but they do help change the feeling of the pattern enough to break the monotony. Try mixing them up.

Another thing: For certain chords you will want to alter the bass pattern (for instance, I use 6-4-6-4- with the G chord, and 4-3-5-3- with the D), and when you are playing melodies, you will find that your middle and index fingers will have to shift to the 2nd and 3rd strings to pick the right melody note.

Railroad Bill and Freight Train are the two most popular picking pieces to learn by, so let's see how they're done. **

Railroad Bill

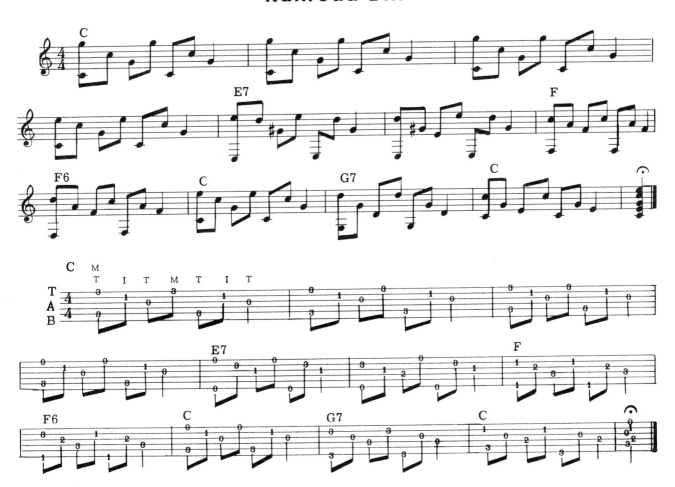

Many people who play steel-string guitars like to use fingerpicks, both to enhance the sound of the guitar and to save wear and tear on the fingernails. There are many varieties of picks on the market, but I recommend a plastic thumb-pick and National brand fingerpicks, which are metal and usually go on the index and middle fingers, of the right hand. The metal picks can be adjusted to the size of your finger easily. Some people prefer plastic fingerpicks, which are softer and have a quiter tone. It is largely a matter of individual taste, and you should experiment with them until you find what is right for you.

Fingerpicks always feel clumsy at first, and the temptation is to immediately throw them away as an unnecessary bother. If you stick with them however, it will soon become as easy to play with them as without them, and the advantages they afford you will be worth the effort.

** These tunes are not transcribed from the recordings by Hobart Smith, or Elizabeth Cotten. Rather, they are simplified as illustrations of this particular style of picking. Compare the pattern picking with the freer styles used by the artists mentioned.

Freight Train

Another pattern that is especially effective for song accompaniment is the one that Peggy Seeger occasionally uses when she is singing a quiet song or ballad. It is based on Elizabeth Cotten's unusual style:

10

Shady Grove, Pastures of Plenty, Nine Hundred Miles, and Blowing in the Wind, are just a few of the songs that work well with this strum.

Now go back to Skip to My Lou, and compare the two approaches to picking. Try playing other simple melodies, mixing the "pattern picking" with the freer style, until there is a synthesis of the two, and an ease with which the bass and the melody line fit together.

One of my favorite songs (Make Me A Pallet on Your Floor) goes beautifully with this style of picking. The more complex chord progression and melody line make this a good song to learn from. It goes like this:

Make Me A Pallet

I'd be more than satisfied,
If I could catch that train and ride,
If I reach Atlanta with no place to go,
Make me a pallet on your floor.

Gonna give everybody my regards,
Even if I have to ride the rods,
If I reach Atlanta with no place to go,
Make me a pallet on your floor.

Let's start picking this one the way we started Skip To My Lou, with a steady bass and a straight, unsyncopated, melody line.

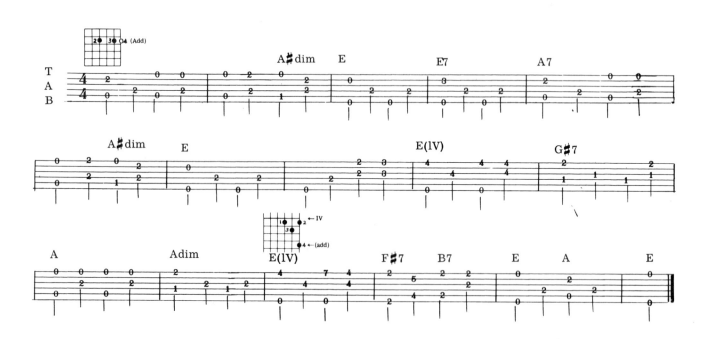

Now we'll start swinging it, by putting some melody notes off the beat. Remember the steady bass!

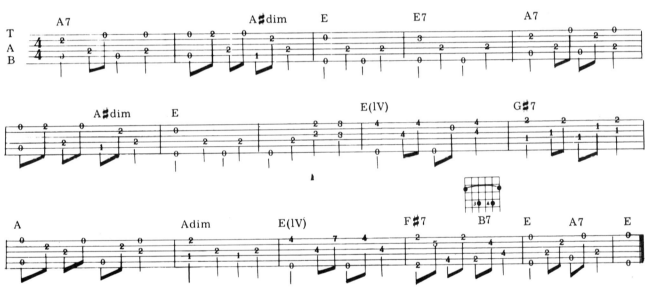

Finally, let's add the ingredients that make this a finished (if there is such a thing) picking piece: some pattern picking, hammer-ons, bass runs, etc. plus anything you feel like throwing in.

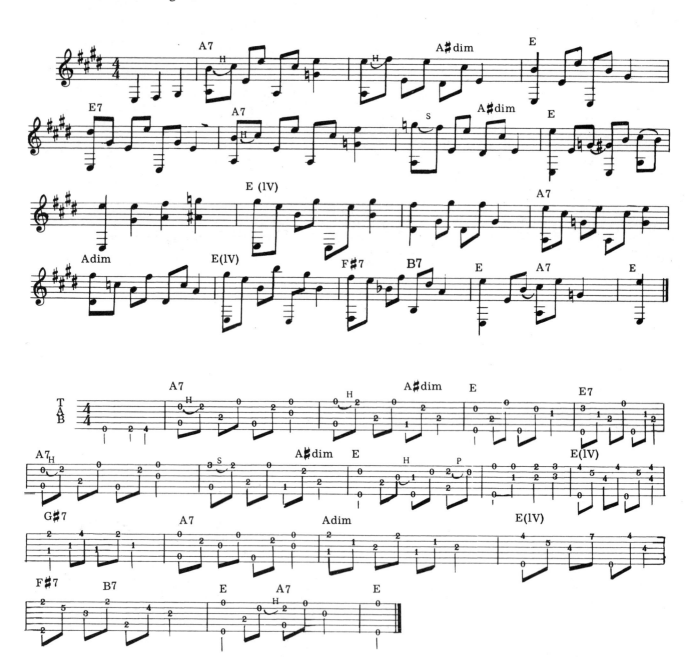

Once you are comfortable with these concepts, start making your way through the pieces transcribed on the following pages. They are arranged more or less in order of difficulty, so if you haven't any burning interest in one particular tune, work your way through from the beginning. If you already fingerpick, of course, start anywhere. Each piece will make a valuable contribution to your own style and technique.

Mississippi John Hurt

Until recently, Mississippi John Hurt's singing and picking was known only to a few folk music and blues enthusiasts who had heard his old Okeh 78's, made in 1928. In the thirty-five years between 1928 and 1963 he lived in obscurity in Mississippi, until he was sought out and rediscovered by Tom Hoskins, a collector and field researcher. He is now one of the most popular blues singer-guitarists, performing at universities, folk festivals, etc., and is admired widely for his distinctive guitar style and warm personality.

Spike Driver's Blues

Spike Driver's Blues has been a favorite of many blues enthusiasts since it was re-released by Folkways as part of their fine Anthology of American Folk Music. It is typical of Mississippi John Hurt's guitar style - an uncomplicated melody line syncopated against a steady 4/4 bass. The entire melody is based on one chord - in this arrangement it is the G chord - and that chord is fingered throughout the piece in the following way:

Sometimes the 4th finger will fret the 2nd or 3rd string, or the 1st finger the 1st string 1st fret (making a G7), but the basic pattern is that of the G. As in all of these picking styles, the most important thing is keeping the thumb going on a steady bass, unchanged by what the treble is doing.

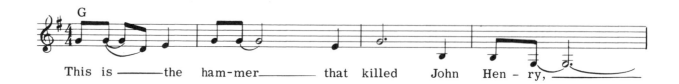

This is ——— the ham-mer——— that killed John Hen - ry, ———

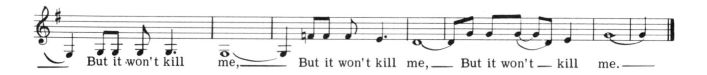

But it won't kill me,—— But it won't kill me,— But it won't — kill me. ——

Take this hammer and carry it to the captain,
Tell him I'm gone (3X)
Take this hammer and carry it to the captain,
Tell him I'm gone, tell him I'm gone,
I'm sure he's gone.

It's a long way from East Colorado,
Honey to my home (3X)
It's a long ways to East Colorado,
Honey to my home, Honey to my home,
That's where I'm goin'.

This is the hammer that killed John Henry,
But it won't kill me (3X)

John Henry he left his hammer,
Laying side the road (3X)

John Henry was a steel-drivin' boy,
But he went down, but he went down,
That's where I'm goin'.

16

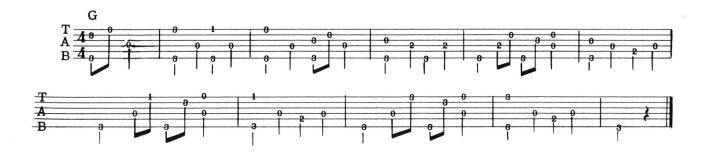

MISSISSIPPI JOHN HURT AT NEWPORT, 1964

Photo by Dave Gahr

My Creole Belle

This is another of Mississippi John Hurt's easy-going, clear-cut pieces. It swings along quietly and simply, but, as in all of his work, there is a real beauty in that quiet simplicity.

You'll notice that in a couple of places he leaves out bass notes, (meas. 5 and 13) which, to me, points up the steady bass even more.

In this and other pieces in this book, the F chord is best played like this

using your thumb for the bass F (6th string 1st fret). When you need a C (5th string 3rd fret), your third finger can shift from the 4th to the 5th string. Your pinky is then free to play the extra notes on the 3rd, 2nd, or 1st strings needed in many of these tunes. (See meas. 3 and 11 in this piece.)

If you absolutely cannot get that thumb over the top of the neck to fret the 6th string, use the standard barre chord instead. (A classical guitarist will tell you this is the only way.)

This song is on Mississippi John Hurt's Piedmont Album called Folk Songs and Blues.

When stars shine, I'll call her mine
My darlin' baby, my Creole Belle.

My Creole Belle, I love her well,
My darlin' baby, my Creole Belle.

Tom Paley

In the late '40's, when the urban folksong movement was just getting under way, a few young city people were deeply involved in studying the traditional instrumental styles of the country. Tom Paley became one of the best guitar and banjo pickers in the city, and was the inspiration of many many other aspiring folk musicians.

Tom played and sang, took photographs, and taught college math throughout the '50's, until he, John Cohen, and Mike Seeger joined forces to form the New Lost City Ramblers in 1958. He is now somewhere in Scandinavia with Claudia, his wife.

Stackerlee

Tom Paley's Stackerlee is based on a combination of Mississippi John Hurt's and
Furry Lewis' versions of the song. Tom throws in his own picking style and out comes
a beautiful guitar piece.

Tom tunes his 6th string down to a D for this one. It can be heard on The New Lost
City Rambler's Volume 4, Folkways FA2399.

Well I re-mem-ber one Sep-tem-ber, on a Fri-day
night, Stack-er-lee— and Bil-ly Lyons— had a great fight.
He's a bad— man, Oh cru-el Stack-er-lee—

You may talk about your gamblers. You ought to see that Richard Lee.
Shot a hundred dollars and he came out on a three
REFRAIN: (After each verse)
    He's a bad man. Oh cruel Stackerlee.

Stack he says to Billy, "You can't play like that.
You won all my money, now you're trying to get my Stetson hat".

Billy, he shot six bits. Stack, he bet he passed.
Stack he out with his .45, says "You done shot your last".

"Oh, Mr. Stackerlee, please don't take my life.
I've got three children and a darling loving wife".

"God'll take care of your children; I'll take care of your wife.
You took my Stetson hat, now I'm gonna take your life."

A woman come a-running, fell upon her knees.
"Oh, Mr. Stackerlee, don't shoot my brother, please".

Woman says to the sheriff, "How can that be?"
You can arrest everybody but you're scared of Stackerlee.

The judge says to the sheriff, "Want him dead or alive."
"Well, how in the world can I bring him in when he totes a .45?"

Stack says to the jailer, "Jailer, I can't sleep,
'Cause all around my bedside Billy Lyons begins to creep".

Two o'clock next Tuesday, upon a scaffold high,
People coming from miles around just to watch old Stackerlee die.

And down in New Orleans there's a place called the Lions Club,
Where every step you take you're stepping in Billy Lyons' blood.

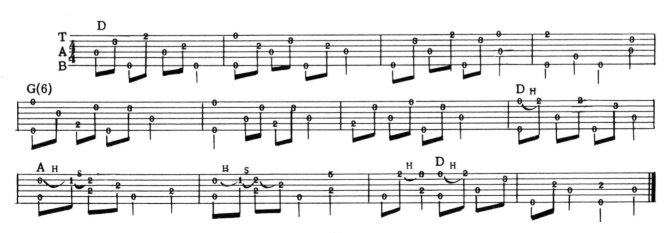

Etta Baker

Etta Baker is not nearly as well known to city audiences as she should be. She has never performed in the North, and her only recording is an important but little heard album called Instrumental Music of the Southern Appalachians. (Tradition Records - TLP 1007) Her style is strong and distinctive, and I strongly urge anyone who is interested in finger picking styles to listen to her.

Bully of the Town

This piece is the first one in this book in which the thumb does more than just alternating the bass notes. Here, the thumb plays chords too, in much the same way as it played the bass notes. Instead of picking a single bass string, however, it now brushes across two, three, or four strings at once. The thumb still keeps up that steady 4/4 beat, but now it might be bass-chord-bass-chord, or bass-chord-bass-bass, as it is in various places in Bully of the Town.

Although there are specific chords in the transcriptions, it is never really specific when actually played. Just brush down approximately where the designated notes should be, and don't worry too much about the exact notes of the chord.

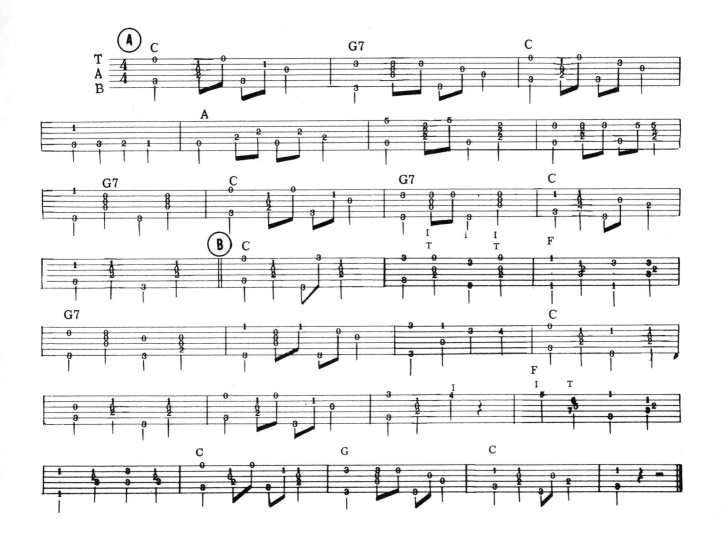

John Henry

Tune your guitar to an open D chord like this: Lower the 6th string one whole tone to a D. This should be an octave lower than the open 4th string. Now do the same to the 1st string, so that is is an octave higher than the 4th string. Now lower the 3rd (G) string one half step so that it is an F#. (You can check it against the 4th string 4th fret.) Next, lower your 2nd string (B) one whole step to an A (one octave higher than your 5th string) and you have an open D chord - D A D F# A D.

Etta Baker's John Henry is played with only one chord throughout the piece. However, there are several tricky slides and syncopations to watch out for.

She plays this as a "knife blues"; that is instead of fretting the guitar in the usual way, she slides a jack-knife blade lightly across the strings, getting that whining, dobro-like sound that so many great blues guitarists get. (A bottle neck or a metal fountain pen top can be used instead of a knife blade.) It usually takes some experimenting before you can get the right sound. If you don't like the sound of "knife blues", you can always revert to the more usual fretting techniques.

Open D tuning-Knife Blues

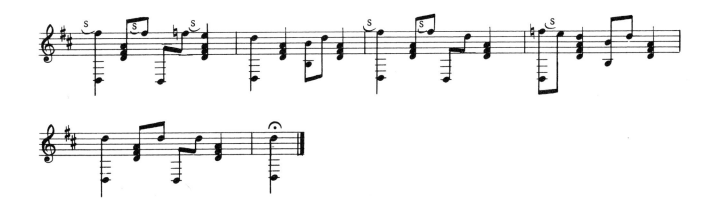

Sam McGee

Sam McGee, along with his brother Kirk, come from Tennessee, and have been singing and picking old-time string music for over forty years. They still have the exuberance and good humor that has made them so popular over the years on Nashville's <u>Grand Ole Opry</u>. They were best known as members of Uncle Dave Macon's Fruit Jar Drinkers in the 'twenties and 'thirties, and later as the Dixieliners, with Fiddlin' Arthur Smith.

Buckdancer's Choice

This transcription was taken from a recent Folkways recording of The McGee Brothers and Arthur Smith (FA2379). Buckdancer's Choice, though, has been a favorite of city guitar pickers since Tom Paley learned it from an early record of Sam McGee and recorded it himself. This tune has been played and "folk-processed" so much that many people will be surprised to hear what the original sounds like.

The bass pattern varies between bass-bass and bass-chord. This changes in the first two measures of the B section, where the melody is played by the thumb. The index finger brushes down across the top three strings for the chord.

Photo by Jerry Stevens Courtesy of Folkways Records

Elizabeth Cotten

As a young girl, Elizabeth Cotten played the guitar, but gave it up as she got older. It was much later, when she was working for the Seeger family in Washington, that she was "discovered" by Mike, who was just learning to play at the time. "Mike handed her the guitar and a myriad of notes began rippling forth to what must have been an amazed and awestruck Mike. I don't know that <u>Freight Train</u> was the first piece that Libba played for Mike, but, if it wasn't the first, it was soon to come, and it immediately became the piece that you identified with Libba."*

*Ed Badeaux - <u>Sing Out</u>! Sept. 1964.

Spanish Flang Dang

This piece is different in many ways from the others in this collection. For one thing, the guitar is tuned to an open G chord. The 6th and 1st strings are tuned down one whole step to D (as in the D tuning), and the 5th string is also dropped one whole tone to G, so that you have D G D G B D. The C chord is made by barring the fifth fret, and the D by barring the seventh (see section D). The D7 chord is formed like this:

Another way that this tune is different is that it is in waltz time. In fact, it doesn't sound at all like a folk tune, but more like an adaptation of a classical piece. It has many other names (most often called the Spanish Fandango) and was probably used mainly for dancing. Whatever it is, it's a lovely tune, and Elizabeth Cotten weaves a spell with it.

A chord with a wiggly line next to it should be "rolled" slightly, by letting your thumb strum down the strings so that each note is heard, rather than hearing them all simultaneously. The first finger then picks the melody note at the end of the "roll". (It is best to listen to the record to get the exact sound).

I find the best right hand fingering to be: T I T
                                         M

From Negro Folksongs and Tunes - Folkways FG 3526

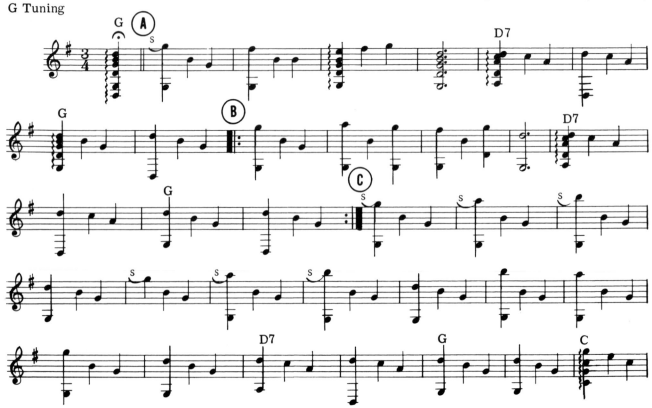

Wilson Rag

Elizabeth Cotten is best known for her song <u>Freight Train,</u> and through it she has influenced countless numbers of guitar pickers and folk singers. (See Ed Badeaux' transcription in Sing Out! Vol. 14 #4). Less known, but certainly as valuable, are many of her other songs and guitar pieces on the Folkways Album <u>Negro Folksongs and Tunes</u> (FG 3526).

<u>Wilson Rag</u> is one that has intrigued me for a long time. It has unusual chord changes and intricate right-hand picking patterns that make it much more interesting than many other similar tunes. It starts out with a D7+9 chord, which is not nearly as frightening as it sounds. If you move a C7 chord up two frets, and leave the E string open, you have it. In diagram form, it looks like this

Most of the G chords you'll be playing will be fretted in the F position, moved up to the third fret:

Elizabeth Cotten uses a two-finger picking style, but I find it a lot easier using three - Thumb, Index, and Middle. However, you can decide for yourself how you want to do it, as long as that thumb keeps the beat going.

Arranged and adapted by Elizabeth Cotten
© Copyright 1958 by Stormking Music Inc.
All Rights Reserved. Used by Permission.

Merle Travis

The term "Travis picking" has come to represent just about every picking style in our folk heritage, and yet the picking that most people do is not very much like the guitar style of Merle Travis. His style certainly derives from folk sources, yet there is something else there, too. Merle Travis is a modern sophisticated musician, and his thorough study of his instrument has led him to use many jazz and pop guitar techniques while playing folk and "country" music. This gives his playing a unique sound that few folk guitarists can duplicate. He usually uses an electric guitar, and by damping the bass strings with the palm of his right hand, (that is, dulling the strings by touching them very lightly after picking them), he gets a very swingy, modern sound. Compare the feeling of freedom he gets to the more restricted "pattern picking" that usually bears his name.

Nine-Pound Hammer

One of Travis' best known pieces is his arrangement of Nine-Pound Hammer. * You will notice that the thumb occasionally picks more than one string, getting a bass-chord-bass-chord effect.

This nine pound ham- mer, ——— It's a lit - tle too heav - y, ——— for my ——— size, ——— Bud- dy, ——— Bud- dy for my ——— size.

(Chorus) Roll on bud - dy, ——— Don't ya roll so slow, ——— How can I roll, Bud - dy, when the wheels won't go. ———

This nine pound hammer,
It killed John Henry
But it Can't kill me, buddy,
No it can't kill me.

This nine pound hammer
It rings like silver
Shines like gold, buddy,
Shines like gold.

I'm goin' on the mountain
Gonna see my baby
But I ain't a-comin' back, buddy,
No I ain't a-comin' back.

*Because we could not get permission from Travis' publisher to transcribe his song from the record, this is an arrangement I made to give the student as good an idea of Travis' style as possible under the circumstances. The song as played by Merle Travis can be heard on Merle Travis Back Home, Capitol T891. -HT

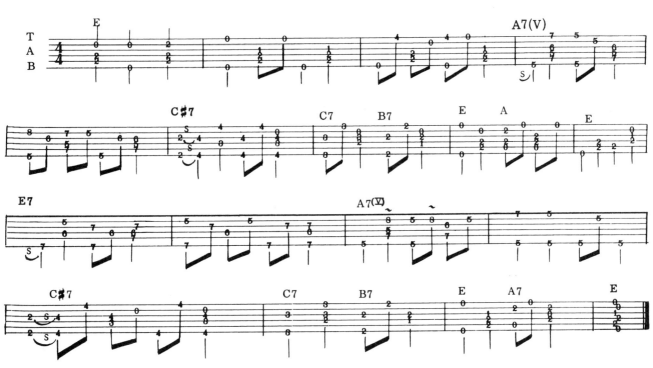

Photo by Dave Gahr

Doc Watson

Doc Watson is from the Blue Ridge Mountains, and his singing and playing are obviously a part of a living tradition, one that is so solid that the generations that helped build that tradition are felt almost as if they are there with him. At the same time, there is always something new happening in Doc's music, and the modern world is very much a part of it.

Doc is technically a virtuoso on every instrument he plays, but it is especially the guitar that comes alive in his hands, speaking in rich and sparkling clean tones. He plays with incredible accuracy, yet never at the expense of subtlety and musicality.

Doc Watson is a superb story teller, and whether he chooses to tell it in a long traditional ballad, an unaccompanied hymn, or an instrumental solo, he always communicates what he has to say to his listeners.

Sitting on Top of the World

Sitting On Top Of The World is played in an open D tuning (DADF#AD). The G chord is made by barring across the fifth fret.

The A7 is made like this:

Doc Watson is at home with flat-picking and finger-picking, and is equally amazing at both. His finger-picking style is very similar to Merle Travis', whose music was a strong influence on Doc's playing.

Doc uses a two-finger right-hand style (thumb and index), as does Rev. Gary Davis and Elizabeth Cotten. I would suggest, however, that the student use three fingers, which are a little more versatile in the hands of us ordinary mortals.

From: Doc Watson - Vanguard VRS-9152

She called me up from down in El Paso
She said, "Come back daddy, I needs you so."
And now she's gone, and I don't worry,
A-Lord I'm sitting on top of the world.

(If) you don't like my peaches, don't you shake
　my tree,
Get out of my orchard, let my peaches be.
And now she's gone, and I don't worry,
A-Lord I'm sitting on top of the world.

And don't you come here running, holding out
　your hand
I'm gonna get me a woman like you got your man.
And now she's gone, and I don't worry,
A-Lord I'm sitting on top of the world.

'Twas in the Spring, one sunny day,
My sweetheart left me, Lord, she went away.
And now she's gone, and I don't worry,
A-Lord I'm sitting on top of the world.

Open D tuning

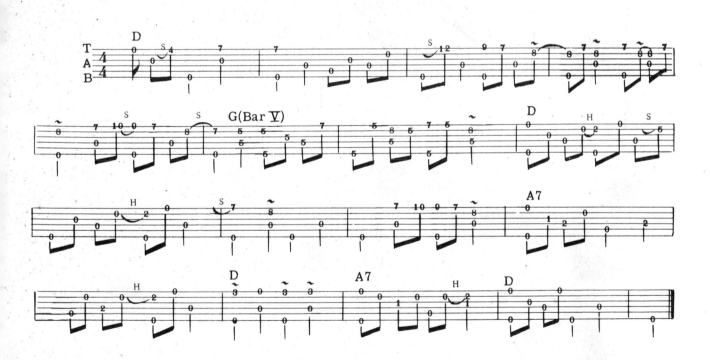

Photo Courtesy of Samuel Charters from John Steiner

Blind Lemon Jefferson

Blind Lemon Jefferson sang and played his guitar in the streets and sporting houses in and around Dallas in the late 1920's. Most of his recordings were on early paramount "race records", many of which have been reissued on two lps by Riverside Records. Anyone interested in folk guitar styles, especially blues, should listen carefully to these recordings. Blind Lemon has, over the years, remained one of the most technically complex, and emotionally moving, of the country blues singers.

The most detailed account of Blind Lemon's life has been written by Sam Charters in The Country Blues, published by Rhinehart and Co. 1959.

49

Bad Luck Blues

In selecting the material for this book, I have purposely stayed away from the field of "blues guitar". Although most blues guitarists use a finger style of playing, it is essentially very different, both rhythmically and harmonically, from the type of picking transcribed here, and deserves a separate and quite different treatment. As in all folk music, however, there is much overlapping, and Blind Lemon's Bad Luck Blues fall into both categories.

The song itself is a twelve-bar blues (with rather unusual phrasing), but the accompaniment that Blind Lemon uses is a type of picking similar to many of the other songs in this book. (Compare it to Candy Man, My Creole Belle, and the first section of St. Louis Tickle.) The main difference is that Blind Lemon's thumb does not keep that steady beat, but uses his bass more sparingly, giving a freer and more subtle effect.

This piece is used as a harmony and counterpoint to the song, and must be learned thoroughly before you attempt to sing with it.

It was learned from The Classic Blues of Blind Lemon Jefferson, Riverside (RLP 12-125)

I bet my money and I lost it, Lord, it's gone
Doggone my bad luck soul,
Mmmmm- lost it, Lord it's gone,
I mean I lost it - years ago,
I ain't never gonna bet on that queen of spades no more.

Well, my good gal left town, why don't you quit cryin'
Doggone my bad luck soul;
Mmmmm- why don't you quit cryin'
Why don't you quit, I mean cryin'
That joker stole off with that long-haired gal of mine.

Sugar, you catch the Katie, and I'll catch that Santa Fe
Doggone my bad luck soul;
You catch the Katie, I'll catch the Santa Fe
I mean the Santa - sing about Fe
When you get to Denver, pretty mama, look around for me.

The woman I love is five feet from the ground
Doggone my bad luck soul;
Hey, five feet from the ground,
Hey, five feet from the - I mean ground,
She's a tailor made woman, she ain't no hand me down.

I ain't seen my sugar in three long weeks today
Doggone my bad luck soul;
I ain't seen my sugar in three long weeks today,
Three long weeks to- I mean day,
God, it's been so long, seems like my heart's gonna break.

I'm goin' on crosstown, catch that southbound Santa Fe
Doggone my bad luck soul;
Mmmm- Lord that Santa Fe,
I mean Santa - sing about Fe,
Be on my way to what you call lovin' Tennessee.

Pete Seeger

More than any other person in the field, Pete Seeger has helped bridge the gap between the traditional music of the country folk and the city folksinger. For years he has been not just a performer, but a teacher and cultural ambassador, bringing a respect for country people and their music to the city, and opening a way for them to come to the cities and universities to teach us what they know.

Aside from his many other well-known talents, Pete has written several guitar instrumental solos, many of which, like his songs, have become standard repetoire in the folk field.

Living in the Country

So far, we have seen how important the steady bass is to the finger-picking style, but Pete Seeger's Living in the Country shows us that variations in the bass can give us subtle changes in accent and emphasis that an unvaried bass lacks. In order to play this one you're going to have to unlearn some of the strict rhythmic patterns that you've spent so much time trying to master.

The 6th string is tuned down to D in this piece. All of the right hand picking is notated by the letters over the tablature. The ring finger (R) is optional, and those notes can be played by the middle finger.

This tune can be heard on <u>Nonesuch And Other Folk Tunes</u> (Folkways FA 2439).

By Pete Seeger
© Copyright 1962, 1963 by FALL RIVER MUSIC INC.
All Rights Reserved. Used by Permission.

Dave Van Ronk

I first heard Dave Van Ronk sing in 1955. It was on a warm Sunday in Washington Square, and, from the opposite side of the park, came the loudest, most raucus sounds I had ever heard. I had to investigate. What I saw was a rather large young man, (possibly bearded, I can't remember,) flailing mercilessly on an old guitar and singing <u>St. James Infirmary</u> at the top of his seemingly indefatigable lungs. Dave was at the beginning of his musical evolution into becoming one of the first, and most influential, of the urban white blues singers.

St. Louis Tickle

This guitar arrangement of an old ragtime piano tune is probably the most difficult piece in this collection, not because of the picking techniques as much as the left hand stretches and unusual fingerings. Dave uses his left thumb quite a bit to fret the 6th and even the 5th string. This is no mean feat, unless you have a pretty big hand or a pretty thin guitar neck, or both. The places in which the bass notes are fretted by the thumb are noted by a small T next to that bass note. Thus, in the first measures, the bass run that opens the piece and the bass notes that accompany the descending melody line (meas. 2) are plucked with the right hand thumb and fretted with the left hand thumb. The F chord, as in several other tunes in this book, is played with the thumb on the 6th string 1st fret, the D7+9 on the 6th string 2nd fret, etc.

The C7 in the B section is fretted like this:

The most difficult part will probably be the C section, where the thumb holds down the G (6th string 3rd fret) while the 2nd and 3rd fingers play the 6th and 7th frets. Fortunately, each beat brings the fingers and thumb closer to a much-needed reunion. Anyhow, it looks like this on paper:

The C that follows is played in the F position with the thumb playing the bass C (6th string 8th fret).

Other chords that you'll have to know are:

F dim   Am7   G7+9   C dim   A♭

Despite its difficulties, this is a worthwhile piece to try to master, and there's a lot going on in it. You should hear Dave's flowing, sensitive rendition on his Prestige album In The Tradition, or the Mercury Dave Van Ronk's Jug Stompers.

Photo by Fritz Richmond Courtesy of Elektra Records

Joseph Spence

Joseph Spence is, unfortunately, known to very few people in this country. He was here for the first time this year to do a series of concerts of music of the Bahamas for the Newport Foundation, but aside from this brief tour he can only be heard on records. Both Folkways and Elektra have recorded him.

Joseph Spence is a musical phenomenon. He plays in a picking style that utilizes traditional tunes, but that is not a traditional style of the Bahamas. His music is very complex, with odd rhythms, counter-melodies, and jazzy variations that seem to come from an endless source of invention. He plays music from many traditions, including American popular music, old hymns, dance tunes, spirituals, and folk songs of the Bahamas.

There Will Be A Happy Meeting

There Will Be A Happy Meeting was transcribed from the Folkways record, Music of the Bahamas, Vol. 1 (FS3844). It is a record that should be carefully listened to by anyone interested in guitar picking styles.

As in all of the guitar pieces on the record, Spence starts with a simple exposition of the melody, and then repeats it, each time improvising a variation of the original theme. I have transcribed below the first five of Spence's variations. It is up to you to continue, with ideas of your own.

Photo by Fritz Richmond Courtesy of Elektra Records

D Tuning